D0590290

# "Excuse me"

## LEARNING ABOUT POLITENESS

### Brian Moses and Mike Gordon

WAYLAND

The VALUES series:

"EXCUSE ME" LEARNING ABOUT **POLITENESS**
"I DON'T CARE!" LEARNING ABOUT **RESPECT**
"I'LL DO IT!" TAKING **RESPONSIBILITY**
"IT WASN'T ME!" LEARNING ABOUT **HONESTY**

Editor: Sarah Doughty
Designer: Malcolm Walker

First published in 1997 by
Wayland Publishers Ltd
61 Western Road, Hove
East Sussex BN3 1JD

Find Wayland on the internet at http:/www.wayland.co.uk

**British Library Cataloguing in Publication Data**
Moses, Brian, 1950 –
"Excuse me": learning about politeness. – (Values)
1. Courtesy – Juvenile literature 2. Etiquette – Juvenile literature
I. Title  II. Gordon, Mike, 1948 –
177.1

ISBN 0 7502 2094 5

Printed and bound by G.Canale & C.S.p.A., Turin

# CONTENTS

How polite are you?
When was the last time
you forgot your manners?

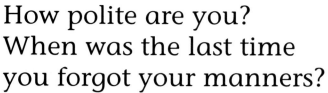

Was it lunchtime?

Was it yesterday when you didn't
give up your seat on the bus?

Was it last week when you were rude to mum's friend?

Or was it last year when you were much smaller and couldn't possibly be expected to behave properly ...

Let's just see how polite you really are.
Do you always remember to say 'please' and 'thank you' or do you sometimes behave like this ...

If you always try to say 'please' and 'thank you' then other people will know that you are grateful for what they do.

Thank you Mrs. Ford, that was a lovely tea.

7

You should always have good
manners at the meal table.

Ask someone to pass you
what you need, don't
make a grab for it.

Eat your food quietly, don't slurp
your soup.

Parents are fond of saying, 'Stop showing off'.

Sometimes this can happen at the meal table when visitors call for tea.

Sometimes it happens
when adults are talking.

Your parents will want to know that you have been behaving politely at school. Do not shout:

Can I go to the toilet; I'm desperate!

If you want to speak to your teacher remember to say 'please' and 'thank you' and ask quietly.

When you visit your friend's house to play, what do you take with you?

Your coat

Your bag

Your favourite toy ...

... Remember to share things, take turns, don't snatch ...

And don't forget your manners!

15

And if you're staying the night at your friend's house, you should be on your best behaviour.

I'll wait, Mr. Johnson, Toby can have his bath first.

Good manners are important if you are invited to someone's party ...

Not everyone can win a prize ... so don't throw a tantrum if you don't win the first game you play.

18

Just be patient and your turn
may come later.

When the party is over it is important to behave
properly ...

Don't grab the party bag and rush out.

Make sure that you thank
your hosts for inviting you
to the party and tell them
that you enjoyed yourself.

Sometimes you might be invited to do something and be unable to go.

If this happens, you should refuse the invitation politely ...

Can you come on holiday with me this year? We're going to the seaside!

Don't hurt someone's feelings by saying that you'll be having a much more exciting time at Disneyland.

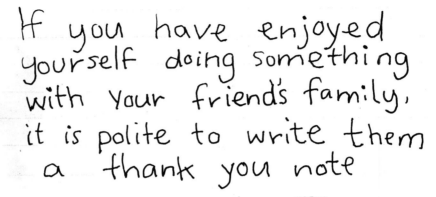

If you have enjoyed yourself doing something with your friend's family, it is polite to write them a thank you note

Tell them how much you enjoyed yourself and how pleased you were to be invited.

You might even feel that you'd like to buy them a thank-you gift.

You should always be polite too when you are given a present yourself, even if it is something you already have ...

And even if it's something you don't really want ...

Be grateful for it.

Thank you, I'm sure it will be useful.

There's a lot to remember when it comes to being polite. How well do you do?

If you are polite, people remember you for all the right reasons.

So wherever you go, whatever you do ... don't forget your manners.

# NOTES FOR PARENTS AND TEACHERS

Prior to reading this book, ask children for examples of what they consider to be good and bad manners. Then read the book with children either individually or in groups and ask them the questions on page 4, 'When did you last forget your manners?' Talk about the answers that you receive. Develop these further by asking children to remember how people reacted to their bad manners. How did children feel about their bad behaviour after the event?

Children might like to act out some of the scenes in the book showing what happens when manners are forgotten. The scene could then be worked on again and changed so that we see how it develops when good manners are put into practice.

Compose rhymes or slogans with the children that remind them that manners are important. These could be read aloud along with hand claps or percussion instruments. For example:

Remember your 'pleases' (*four claps*)
Remember your 'thank yous' (*four claps*)
Remember your 'sorrys' (*four claps*)
These words make good children (*clap on each syllable*)

Talk about appropriate behaviour when at parties, visiting friends' houses, staying the night and so on. Ask children for their own anecdotes. Can they compose a list of rules regarding good manners that would apply to these situations?

Some children might like to write party invitations while others could compose polite letters of refusal. Others could act out phone conversations where they have to politely refuse an invitation to take part in a trip.

Ask children to illustrate the reminder 'Don't forget your manners'. Perhaps it will be a suitcase that's full of polite words, or maybe they'll think of another idea.

Explore manners further through the sharing of picture books mentioned in the book list.

# BOOKS TO READ

*'I Want My Dinner'* by Tony Ross (Collins Picture Lions)
The Little Princess learns some manners but once she has mastered 'please' and 'thank you' she discovers that not everyone else is so well-mannered.

*'Max and the Magic Word'* by Colin and Jacqui Hawkins (Picture Puffin)
Max knows what he wants but not how to get it so his friends have to teach him polite behaviour.

*'The Elephant and the Bad Baby'* by Elfrida Vipont, illustrated by Raymond Briggs (Picture Puffin)
A tale about a baby who never says please.

*'The Bad-Tempered Ladybird'* by Eric Carle (Picture Puffin)
The bad-tempered ladybird is mean, rude and always trying to start a fight but finally learns that it really pays to be polite.

*'When Mum Turned into a Monster'* by Joanna Harrison (Collins Picture Lions)
A look at what can happen when children don't behave around the home. Their rowdy behaviour makes mum so furious that she turns into a monster!

# INDEX